Copyright © 2017   Bruce Speidel
Cover Design © Bruce Speidel
Cover Image "Foundations" painted by Bruce Speidel
All rights reserved

Photo Reference - Chelsea Speidel,
wife of Bruce's cousin Shawn Speidel,
showing her grandpa Ben Barton studying the Bible

Published by Painted Gate Publishing

www.brucespeidel.com

Scripture taken from the
NEW AMERICAN STANDARD BIBLE®, Copyright ©
1960,1962,1963,1968,1971,1972,1973,1975,1977,1995
by The Lockman Foundation. Used by permission.

THE HOLY BIBLE, NEW INTERNATIONAL VERSION®,
NIV® Copyright © 1973, 1978, 1984, 2011 by Biblica, Inc.®
Used by permission. All rights reserved worldwide.

Scripture taken from the New King James Version®.
Copyright © 1982 by Thomas Nelson.
Used by permission. All rights reserved.

Scripture quotations are from the ESV® Bible
(The Holy Bible, English Standard Version®), copyright © 2001
by Crossway, a publishing ministry of Good News Publishers.
Used by permission. All rights reserved.

In a world of relative truth and foundations of sand, people are desperate to find "what is the Truth", and "what can I count on." God's Word is reliable and it is the Truth. A foundation is something to build on and a life built on the bedrock of God's Word can withstand the storms of life. God's Word is the best foundation.

The benefits of memorizing scripture are limitless. In Isaiah 55:11 it says that the word of God will not return to Him empty. Plant the seed of God's Word in your heart and it will produce fruit for the rest of your life, the good fruit.

101-*"A foundation For Life"* is a book to jump-start a lifestyle of learning more about God and meditating on His Word. It is important to read the Bible along with memorizing God's word. Knowing the context around the verses will give you a better understanding. Just as reading the Bible is important, memorization is important. In Psalms 1 it says "blessed is the man that meditates on God's word day and night." How can you meditate on something you don't know or remember? This is why memorization is important. This book is not comprehensive; there are many great verses that are not included. In the back of the book there are 20 pages left blank for you to put verses that are important to you. This is meant to be a foundation to build upon. Don't stop with 101!

This book is organized in the book order that most Bibles are organized. This should make it "easier" to organize and recall them in your mind and help with memory. By no means does that mean "easy." It will take work.

Memorization can be difficult if you have not practiced it. If it is hard at first, don't lose heart! With consistent practice the "memorization muscles" will develop and it will become easier.

If you have the opportunity, get others involved with scripture memory. Encourage each other and work together. Consider rewards along the way to help encourage, and a special award when your 101 is memorized.

Grandmas, Grandpas, Uncles, Aunts and friends, this could be a great opportunity to encourage young and old Christians in their walk with God. If you cannot be there to teach and memorize with them, you can encourage them by giving them this book and rewarding them as they memorize scripture. The value of God's word planted in a heart is worth every penny!

"Everyone then who hears these words of mine and does them will be like a wise man who built his house on the rock." — Matthew 7:24 ESV

Make God's Word the foundation for your life!

Helpful Methods For Memorization

- One of the best ways to memorize is repeating the verse out-loud as many times as it takes.
- Some people learn best by writing the verse on a separate piece of paper multiple times.
- Pictures. Drawing pictures on the pages that help you connect with the verse can be a big help. For example, Jeremiah 17:9 says that "the heart is deceitful and desperately sick…" on that page you could draw a heart and a thermometer.
- Continuing with pictures, you could draw pictures on the back of flash cards. You can make flash cards with 3x5 note cards, writing scripture on one side and the reference with pictures on the other.
- Actions that go along with verse can be helpful too.

Genesis 1:1 NKJV

In the beginning God created the heavens and the earth.

Genesis 15:6 NIV

Abram believed the Lord, and he credited it to him as righteousness.

Genesis 50:20 NIV

You intended to harm me, but God intended it for good to accomplish what is now being done, the saving of many lives.

Exodus 20:2 NKJV

I *am* the Lord your God, who brought you out of the land of Egypt, out of the house of bondage.

The Ten Commandments
(Exodus 20:1-21)

1. You shall have no other gods before me
2. You shall not make for yourself an idol
3. You shall not misuse the name of the Lord your God
4. Remember the Sabbath and keep it Holy
5. Honor your father and mother
6. You shall not murder
7. You shall not commit adultery
8. You shall not steal
9. You shall not give false testimony
10. You shall not covet

Numbers 23:19 ESV

God is not man, that he should lie,
or a son of man, that he should change his mind.
Has he said, and will he not do it?
Or has he spoken, and will he not fulfill it?

Deuteronomy 31:8 ESV

It is the Lord who goes before you. He will be with you; he will not leave you or forsake you. Do not fear or be dismayed.

Joshua 24:15 NASB

"If it is disagreeable in your sight to serve the Lord, choose for yourselves today whom you will serve: whether the gods which your fathers served which were beyond the River, or the gods of the Amorites in whose land you are living; but as for me and my house, we will serve the Lord."

Esther 4:14 NKJV

"For if you remain completely silent at this time, relief and deliverance will arise for the Jews from another place, but you and your father's house will perish. Yet who knows whether you have come to the kingdom for *such* a time as this?"

Psalm 1:1-3 NKJV

Blessed *is* the man
Who walks not in the counsel of the ungodly,
Nor stands in the path of sinners,
Nor sits in the seat of the scornful;
But his delight *is* in the law of the Lord,
And in His law he meditates day and night.
He shall be like a tree
Planted by the rivers of water,
That brings forth its fruit in its season,
Whose leaf also shall not wither;
And whatever he does shall prosper.

Psalm 32:8 NASB

I will instruct you and teach you in the way which you should go; I will counsel you with My eye upon you.

Psalm 34:6 NKJV

This poor man cried out, and the Lord heard *him*,
And saved him out of all his troubles.

Psalm 103:11-12 NASB

For as high as the heavens are above the earth,
So great is His lovingkindness toward those who fear Him.
As far as the east is from the west,
So far has He removed our transgressions from us.

Psalm 119:105 KJV

Thy word is a lamp unto my feet, and a light unto my path.

Psalm 139:7-10 NIV

Where can I go from your Spirit? Where can I flee from your presence? If I go up to the heavens, you are there; if I make my bed in the depths, you are there. If I rise on the wings of the dawn, if I settle on the far side of the sea, even there your hand will guide me, your right hand will hold me fast.

Proverbs 1:7 NKJV

The fear of the Lord *is* the beginning of knowledge,
But fools despise wisdom and instruction.

Proverbs 3:5-6 NKJV

Trust in the Lord with
all your heart,
And lean not on your
own understanding;
In all your ways
acknowledge Him,
And He shall direct your
paths.

Proverbs 3:7-8 NKJV

Do not be wise in
your own eyes;
Fear the Lord and
depart from evil.
It will be health to
your flesh,
And strength to your
bones.

Proverbs 18:10 NKJV

The name of the Lord *is* a strong tower;
The righteous run to it and are safe.

Proverbs 18:21a NASB

Death and life are in the power of the tongue,

Proverbs 21:31 NASB

The horse is prepared for the day of battle, But victory belongs to the Lord.

Proverbs 22:7b NKJV

the borrower *is* servant to the lender.

Proverbs 25:28 NIV

Like a city whose walls are broken through is a person who lacks self-control.

Ecclesiastes 4:9 NASB

Two are better than one because they have a good return for their labor.

Ecclesiastes 12:13-14 NIV

Now all has been heard; here is the conclusion of the matter: Fear God and keep his commandments, for this is the duty of all mankind. For God will bring every deed into judgment, including every hidden thing, whether it is good or evil.

Isaiah 26:3 NKJV

You will keep *him* in perfect peace,
Whose mind *is* stayed *on You,*
Because he trusts in You.

Isaiah 26:8 NASB

Indeed, *while following* the way of Your judgments, O Lord,
We have waited for You eagerly;
Your name, even Your memory, is the desire of *our* souls.

Isaiah 40:29-31 NIV

He gives strength to the weary and increases the power of the weak. Even youths grow tired and weary, and young men stumble and fall; but those who hope in the Lord will renew their strength. They will soar on wings like eagles; they will run and not grow weary, they will walk and not be faint.

Isaiah 55:10-11 NIV

As the rain and the snow come down from heaven, and do not return to it without watering the earth and making it bud and flourish, so that it yields seed for the sower and bread for the eater, so is my word that goes out from my mouth: It will not return to me empty,
but will accomplish what I desire and achieve the purpose for which I sent it.

Jeremiah 12:5 ESV

"If you have raced with men on foot, and they have wearied you,
how will you compete with horses?
And if in a safe land you are so trusting,
what will you do in the thicket of the Jordan?"

Jeremiah 15:16 ESV

Your words were found, and I ate them, and your words became to me a joy and the delight of my heart,
for I am called by your name,
O Lord, God of hosts.

Jeremiah 17:9 ESV

The heart is deceitful above all things,
and desperately sick;
who can understand it?

Jeremiah 29:11 NIV

"For I know the plans I have for you," declares the Lord, "plans to prosper you and not to harm you, plans to give you hope and a future."

Jeremiah 32:17 KJV

Ah Lord God! behold, thou hast made the heaven and the earth by thy great power and stretched out arm, and there is nothing too hard for thee:

Jeremiah 33:3 ESV

Call to me and I will answer you, and will tell you great and hidden things that you have not known.

Daniel 6:27 NKJV

He delivers and rescues,
And He works signs and wonders
In heaven and on earth,
Who has delivered Daniel from the power of the lions.

Micah 6:8 NKJV

He has shown you, O
man, what *is* good;
And what does the Lord
require of you
But to do justly,
To love mercy,
And to walk humbly
with your God?

Haggai 2:8 NASB

'The silver is Mine and the gold is Mine,' declares the Lord of hosts.

Matthew 3:2 NASB

"Repent, for the kingdom of heaven is at hand."

Matthew 6:33 NASB

But seek first His kingdom and His righteousness, and all these things will be added to you.

Matthew 7:24 ESV

"Everyone then who hears these words of mine and does them will be like a wise man who built his house on the rock."

Matthew 9:37-38 NIV

Then he said to his disciples, "The harvest is plentiful but the workers are few. Ask the Lord of the harvest, therefore, to send out workers into his harvest field."

Matthew 13:44 NIV

"The kingdom of heaven is like treasure hidden in a field. When a man found it, he hid it again, and then in his joy went and sold all he had and bought that field."

Matthew 19:26 ESV

But Jesus looked at them and said, "With man this is impossible, but with God all things are possible."

Matthew 22:37-40 NKJV

Jesus said to him, "'You shall love the Lord your God with all your heart, with all your soul, and with all your mind.' This is *the* first and great commandment. And *the* second *is* like it: 'You shall love your neighbor as yourself.' On these two commandments hang all the Law and the Prophets."

Matthew 28:18-20 NKJV

And Jesus came and spoke to them, saying, "All authority has been given to Me in heaven and on earth. Go therefore and make disciples of all the nations, baptizing them in the name of the Father and of the Son and of the Holy Spirit, teaching them to observe all things that I have commanded you; and lo, I am with you always, *even* to the end of the age." Amen.

Luke 1:38 ESV

And Mary said, "Behold, I am the servant of the Lord; let it be to me according to your word." And the angel departed from her.

Luke 9:23 NASB

And He was saying to *them* all, "If anyone wishes to come after Me, he must deny himself, and take up his cross daily and follow Me.

Luke 12:34 KJV

For where your treasure is, there will your heart be also.

Luke 22:42 NASB

"Father, if You are willing, remove this cup from Me; yet not My will, but Yours be done."

John 3:16-17 NKJV

For God so loved the world that He gave His only begotten Son, that whoever believes in Him should not perish but have everlasting life. For God did not send His Son into the world to condemn the world, but that the world through Him might be saved.

John 5:24 ESV

Truly, truly, I say to you, whoever hears my word and believes him who sent me has eternal life. He does not come into judgment, but has passed from death to life.

John 6:29 NIV

Jesus answered, "The work of God is this: to believe in the one he has sent."

John 8:31b-32 NKJV

"If you abide in My word, you are My disciples indeed. And you shall know the truth, and the truth shall make you free."

John 14:21 NASB

He who has My commandments and keeps them is the one who loves Me; and he who loves Me will be loved by My Father, and I will love him and will disclose Myself to him."

John 15:5 NASB

I am the vine, you are the branches; he who abides in Me and I in him, he bears much fruit, for apart from Me you can do nothing.

John 16:24 NASB

Until now you have asked for nothing in My name; ask and you will receive, so that your joy may be made full.

John 17:3 NASB

This is eternal life, that they may know You, the only true God, and Jesus Christ whom You have sent.

Acts 1:8 ESV

But you will receive power when the Holy Spirit has come upon you, and you will be my witnesses in Jerusalem and in all Judea and Samaria, and to the end of the earth."

Acts 4:11-12 ESV

This Jesus is the stone that was rejected by you, the builders, which has become the cornerstone. And there is salvation in no one else, for there is no other name under heaven given among men by which we must be saved."

Acts 5:42 ESV

And every day, in the temple and from house to house, they did not cease teaching and preaching that the Christ is Jesus.

Acts 10:34-35 ESV

So Peter opened his mouth and said: "Truly I understand that God shows no partiality, but in every nation anyone who fears him and does what is right is acceptable to him.

Romans 3:23 NKJV

for all have sinned and fall short of the glory of God,

Romans 5:3b-5 ESV

But we rejoice in our sufferings, knowing that suffering produces endurance, and endurance produces character, and character produces hope, and hope does not put us to shame, because God's love has been poured into our hearts through the Holy Spirit who has been given to us.

Romans 5:8 NASB

But God demonstrates His own love toward us, in that while we were yet sinners, Christ died for us.

Romans 6:1-2 ESV

What shall we say then? Are we to continue in sin that grace may abound? By no means! How can we who died to sin still live in it?

Romans 6:23 NASB

For the wages of sin is death, but the free gift of God is eternal life in Christ Jesus our Lord.

Romans 10:9-10 NASB

that if you confess with your mouth Jesus *as* Lord, and believe in your heart that God raised Him from the dead, you will be saved; for with the heart a person believes, resulting in righteousness, and with the mouth he confesses, resulting in salvation.

Romans 10:14-15 ESV

How then will they call on him in whom they have not believed? And how are they to believe in him of whom they have never heard? And how are they to hear without someone preaching? And how are they to preach unless they are sent? As it is written, "How beautiful are the feet of those who preach the good news!"

Romans 11:2-4 ESV

God has not rejected his people whom he foreknew. Do you not know what the Scripture says of Elijah, how he appeals to God against Israel? "Lord, they have killed your prophets, they have demolished your altars, and I alone am left, and they seek my life." But what is God's reply to him? "I have kept for myself seven thousand men who have not bowed the knee to Baal."

Romans 12:1-2 NIV

Therefore, I urge you, brothers and sisters, in view of God's mercy, to offer your bodies as a living sacrifice, holy and pleasing to God – this is your true and proper worship. Do not conform to the pattern of this world, but be transformed by the renewing of your mind. Then you will be able to test and approve what God's will is – his good, pleasing and perfect will.

Romans 13:8 NASB

Owe nothing to anyone except to love one another; for he who loves his neighbor has fulfilled *the* law.

1 Corinthians 10:13 NASB

No temptation has overtaken you but such as is common to man; and God is faithful, who will not allow you to be tempted beyond what you are able, but with the temptation will provide the way of escape also, so that you will be able to endure it.

1 Corinthians 13:4-8a NIV

Love is patient, love is kind. It does not envy, it does not boast, it is not proud. It does not dishonor others, it is not self-seeking, it is not easily angered, it keeps no record of wrongs. Love does not delight in evil but rejoices with the truth. It always protects, always trusts, always hopes, always perseveres.
Love never fails.

Galatians 5:22-23 ESV

But the fruit of the Spirit is love, joy, peace, patience, kindness, goodness, faithfulness, gentleness, self-control; against such things there is no law.

Ephesians 2:8-10 NIV

For it is by grace you have been saved, through faith — and this is not from yourselves, it is the gift of God – not by works, so that no one can boast. For we are God's handiwork, created in Christ Jesus to do good works, which God prepared in advance for us to do.

Philippians 2:13 NKJV

for it is God who works in you both to will and to do for *His* good pleasure.

Philippians 4:6-7 NIV

Do not be anxious about anything, but in every situation, by prayer and petition, with thanksgiving, present your requests to God. And the peace of God, which transcends all understanding, will guard your hearts and your minds in Christ Jesus.

Philippians 4:13 NKJV

I can do all things through Christ who strengthens me.

1 Timothy 1:5 NIV

The goal of this command is love, which comes from a pure heart and a good conscience and a sincere faith.

2 Timothy 2:2 NIV

And the things you have heard me say in the presence of many witnesses entrust to reliable people who will also be qualified to teach others.

2 Timothy 3:16-17 NIV

All scripture is God-breathed and is useful for teaching, rebuking, correcting and training in righteousness, so that the servant of God may be thoroughly equipped for every good work.

Hebrews 1:3 ESV

He is the radiance of the glory of God and the exact imprint of his nature, and he upholds the universe by the word of his power. After making purification for sins, he sat down at the right hand of the Majesty on high,

Hebrews 4:12 NIV

For the word of God is alive and active. Sharper than any double-edged sword, it penetrates even to dividing soul and spirit, joints and marrow; it judges the thoughts and attitudes of the heart.

Hebrews 9:27-28 ESV

And just as it is appointed for man to die once, and after that comes judgment, so Christ, having been offered once to bear the sins of many, will appear a second time, not to deal with sin but to save those who are eagerly waiting for him.

Hebrews 10:24-25 NIV

And let us consider how we may spur one another on toward love and good deeds, not giving up on meeting together, as some are in the habit of doing, but encouraging one another – and all the more as you see the Day approaching.

Hebrews 12:1-2 NIV

Therefore, since we are surrounded by such a great cloud of witnesses, let us throw off everything that hinders and the sin that so easily entangles. And let us run with perseverance the race marked out for us, fixing our eyes on Jesus, the pioneer and perfecter of faith. For the joy set before him he endured the cross, scorning its shame, and sat down at the right hand of the throne of God.

Hebrews 13:6 ESV

So we can confidently say,
"The Lord is my helper;
I will not fear;
what can man do to me?"

Hebrews 13:17 NIV

Have confidence in your leaders and submit to their authority, because they keep watch over you as those who must give an account. Do this so that their work will be a joy, not a burden, for that would be of no benefit to you.

James 1:5 NIV

If any of you lacks wisdom, you should ask God, who gives generously to all without finding fault, and it will be given to you.

James 1:19 NIV

My dear brothers and sisters, take note of this: Everyone should be quick to listen, slow to speak and slow to become angry,

James 1:27 NIV

Religion that God our Father accepts as pure and faultless is this: to look after orphans and widows in their distress and to keep oneself from being polluted by the world.

James 4:7 ESV

Submit yourselves therefore to God. Resist the devil, and he will flee from you.

2 Peter 1:3 NASB

seeing that His divine power has granted to us everything pertaining to life and godliness, through the true knowledge of Him who called us by His own glory and excellence.

1 John 1:3 NIV

We proclaim to you what we have seen and heard, so that you also may have fellowship with us. And our fellowship is with the Father and with his Son, Jesus Christ.

1 John 1:9 ESV

If we confess our sins, he is faithful and just to forgive us our sins and to cleanse us from all unrighteousness.

1 John 4:18-19 ESV

There is no fear in love, but perfect love casts out fear. For fear has to do with punishment, and whoever fears has not been perfected in love. We love because He first loved us.

1 John 5:3 NKJV

For this is the love of God, that we keep His commandments. And His commandments are not burdensome

1 John 5:11-13 ESV

And this is the testimony, that God gave us eternal life, and this life is in his Son. Whoever has the Son has life; whoever does not have the Son of God does not have life.

I write these things to you who believe in the name of the Son of God, that you may know that you have eternal life.

Revelation 12:11 NKJV

And they overcame him by the blood of the Lamb and by the word of their testimony, and they did not love their lives to the death.

Revelation 22:20-21 NIV

He who testifies to these things says, "Yes, I am coming soon."
Amen. Come, Lord Jesus.
The grace of the Lord Jesus be with God's people. Amen.

www.ingramcontent.com/pod-product-compliance
Lightning Source LLC
Chambersburg PA
CBHW071520080526
44588CB00011B/1498